THIS AWESOME

FIELD GUIDE

BELONGS

TO

hi! sign your name here ⮫

LOVE LIKE ♡ JESUS

Wait, what's a FIELD GUIDE?
A field guide is a book designed to help
you identify things along a journey.
It's something you take with you to help
you make sense of what's around you.

Live It Out: A Field Guide To Loving Like Jesus
Published by Orange, a division of The reThink Group, Inc.
5870 Charlotte Lane, Suite 300
Cumming, GA 30040

Scriptures taken from the Holy Bible, New International Reader's
Version®, NIrV® Copyright © 1995, 1996, 1998, 2014 by Biblica, Inc.™
Used by permission of Zondervan. www.zondervan.com The "NIrV" and "New
International Reader's Version" are trademarks registered in the United
States Patent and Trademark Office by Biblica, Inc.™

Other Orange products available online and direct from publisher.
Visit our website at www.thinkorange.com for more resources like these.

ISBN: 978-1-63570-234-7
© 2024 The reThink Group, Inc.

Content and Editorial Team: Dan Scott, Danielle Wilkins,
Hannah Joiner Crosby, Leslie Mack, Mike Tiemann
Cover and Interior Design: Elizabeth Hildreth
Illustrations: Studio MUTI

Printed in the United States of America
First Edition 2024
1 2 3 4 5 6 7 8 9 10

09/16/24

A **FIELD GUIDE** TO **LOVING LIKE JESUS**

HEY YOU!

This book you're holding right now is a FIELD GUIDE to the adventure of life!

You do know that you're on an adventure, right? It's true. Just by waking up and living your life, you're journeying into the unknown. And you get to decide HOW you want to live—today and every day! (Whoa.)

That's a big deal. If only you had a really great example to follow...

This is where Jesus comes in.

You see, Jesus wasn't just any person who lived thousands of years ago. Jesus was—and still is—God's Son. His entire life was like a living field guide to show us how to live the life God wants for us. (Plus, on top of that, because of Jesus' life, death, and resurrection, we can experience God's love forever and ever! That's the best part.)

And, yeah. It's true that sometimes when people think of God, they think about:
- ➜ hundreds of rules to follow,
- ➜ complicated words that thou needest to rememorizeth,
- ➜ fancy Sunday clothes you wear into a building once a week just to smile at strangers before you can eat a late lunch...

But that's not the case. Jesus made it clear. The adventure of life can be SO MUCH better than that.

In fact, everything that Jesus said is summed up—not in a list of complicated rules—but in one adventure-filled phrase that Jesus wanted everyone to remember and live by: LOVE ONE ANOTHER.

Jesus said to His disciples:

"I give you a new command. Love one another. You must love one another, just as I have loved you." — John 13:34

See, knowing facts about Jesus is one thing. But if we choose to love the way Jesus invites us to love, THAT changes everything. Get it? We've experienced Jesus' love... and now we get to LIVE IT OUT!

But how? One word: BEATITUDES.

You might think, "You know, that sounds like 'attitude.'" But it's the opposite of rolling your eyes, walking off, or being spicy with your words.

The Beatitudes are a series of phrases that Jesus shared that will help us embrace the challenge to live out His love. As you read, think about this. Each beatitude includes two parts: an action from us, and a response from God.

Here's what Jesus said:

"Blessed are those who are spiritually needy.
   The kingdom of heaven belongs to them.
Blessed are those who are sad.
   They will be comforted.
Blessed are those who are humble.
   They will be given the earth.
Blessed are those who are hungry and thirsty
      for what is right.
   They will be filled.
Blessed are those who show mercy.
   They will be shown mercy.
Blessed are those whose hearts are pure.
   They will see God.
Blessed are those who make peace.
   They will be called children of God.
Blessed are those who suffer for doing what
      is right.
The kingdom of heaven belongs to them."
      — Matthew 5:3-10

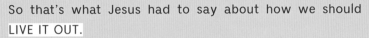

So that's what Jesus had to say about how we should
LIVE IT OUT.

We hope that what you're about to read will help you navigate the adventure of your life as you follow Jesus.

READY TO GET STARTED?

What's Ahead

As you continue through this book, you'll discover several ways that you can live like Jesus by sharing His love. Here's what you'll find in each of the sections ahead:

THE BIG IDEA

A big idea from the apostle Paul about how we can show Jesus' love. (Paul wrote several letters to help people understand what it means to follow Jesus.)

WHAT JESUS SAID

What Jesus said about that same idea.
(Hint: You just read about it in the Beatitudes!)

WHAT JESUS DID

An example of how Jesus Himself lived out that big idea.

THE IDEA IN ACTION

An example of someone else in the Bible who lived out that big idea.

YOUR ADVENTURE

Activities to help you figure out how YOU can live out that idea today. (You can even earn a badge when you complete the activities.)

START YOUR JOURNEY & TURN THE PAGE!

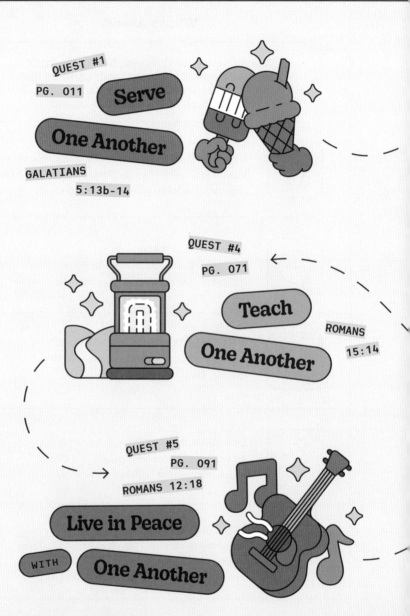

QUEST #1

PG. 011

Serve

One Another

GALATIANS 5:13b-14

QUEST #4

PG. 071

Teach

One Another

ROMANS 15:14

QUEST #5

PG. 091

ROMANS 12:18

Live in Peace

WITH **One Another**

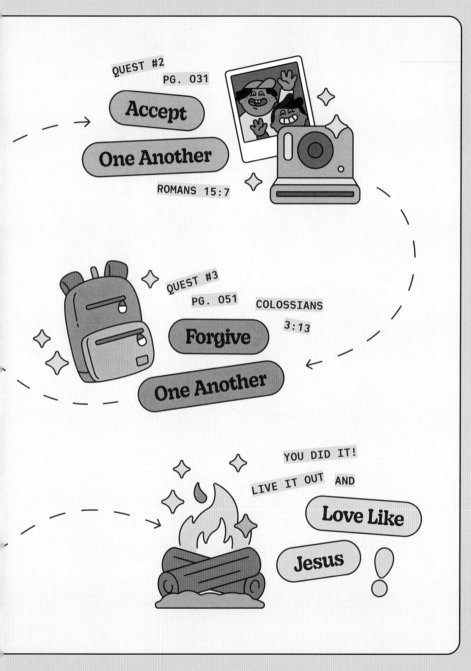

QUEST #2
PG. 031
Accept
One Another
ROMANS 15:7

QUEST #3
PG. 051
COLOSSIANS 3:13
Forgive
One Another

YOU DID IT!
LIVE IT OUT AND
Love Like
Jesus !

GALATIANS 5:13b-14

Serve one another in love. The whole law is fulfilled by obeying this one command. "Love your neighbor as you love yourself."

QUEST

1

Serve

One
Another

SERVE ONE ANOTHER

Can you think of some places where others have served you? Maybe a restaurant, convenience store, or ice cream shop.

Or maybe you've been served at home by a parent or family member. Maybe they made you a meal, kept your room clean, or drove you to basketball practice.

Did you know those are acts of service just like the ones you might receive at a restaurant? Actually... they might even be better because they come from someone who loves you. When a family member or close friend helps you out, they don't do it so they can get a paycheck or some sort of reward... or even a thank-you note. (Though writing them one might be a great idea. Hint-hint.) They serve you—they help you—because they LOVE you.

After Jesus died on the cross, came back to life, and went to be with God, the followers of Jesus looked for ways to put Jesus' love into action. One of those ways turned out to be acts of service.

The apostle Paul wrote about service in a letter to the church he started in Galatia:

Serve one another in love. The whole law is fulfilled by obeying this one command. "Love your neighbor as you love yourself." — Galatians 5:13b-14

In other words, when you serve others, you're LIVING IT OUT! You're living out the love of Jesus and making a difference for the people you've chosen to serve.

Take a few moments and write down some thoughts about these questions:

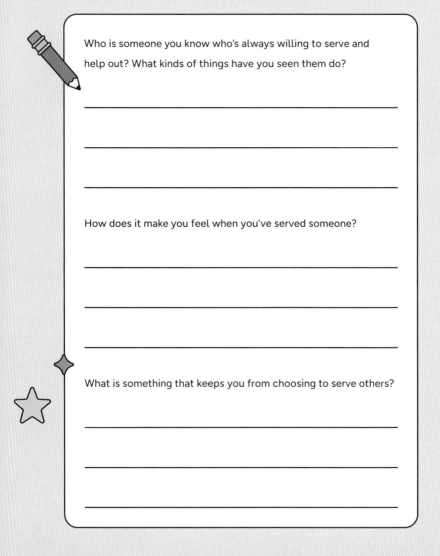

Who is someone you know who's always willing to serve and help out? What kinds of things have you seen them do?

_____

_____

_____

How does it make you feel when you've served someone?

_____

_____

_____

What is something that keeps you from choosing to serve others?

_____

_____

_____

It's time for a fireside chat!

(Okay, maybe not a "real" one.) Take some time to think about someone who's served you and how that made you feel. Fill in the blanks below.

One time, when I was at

> ,

(where were you?)

>

(someone's name)

> .

(what did they do for you?)

I was really

>

(how did it make you feel?)

because

> .

(why did it make you feel that way?)

I felt so loved! I'm grateful for how

>

(the person's name)

served me.

WHAT JESUS SAID...

If we want to follow Jesus and live out His love, we need to pay attention to the things that He said are most important. Jesus reimagined what it looks like to live our lives— not by serving ourselves and getting our own way, but by serving others.

Jesus said: **"Blessed are those who are humble."** — Matthew 5:5a

In this box, write down what you think it means to be humble.

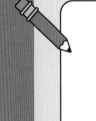

Basically, when you're humble, you think of others more than you think about yourself. You don't think you're too cool to hang out with anyone. Even if you do some great stuff, you choose not to show off or treat others poorly.

It might seem like being humble means being weak, or mild, or even getting overlooked while others get all the success and attention. But actually, people who are humble are incredibly strong. Humility is about the choices you make, with God's help—to use your gifts and talents not just for yourself, but for the good of those around you.

People who are humble are people who are ready to serve. People who aren't humble will miss the chance to serve.

Look again at what Jesus said:

"Blessed are those who are humble.
   They will be given the earth." — Matthew 5:5

Some people try to get more stuff, more power, or more money by putting themselves first and putting other people down. But Jesus said that if you want the most out of life... if you want to REALLY live... choose to be humble.

What matters most is LOVE...
→ being humble.
→ choosing to serve.
→ showing others you care.

Remember this verse.

Memorizing verses from the Bible can help you live more like Jesus each day! Let's put some motions to it and give it a try.

You can do it! Keep practicing by showing a parent or family member.

01: Raise both hands up high

"Blessed

are those

02: Point to others, then point to yourself

03: Palms open in front of you

who are humble.

They

04: Point to others, then point to yourself

05: Cup both of your hands together

will be given

the earth."

06: Make a big circle with both index fingers

07: Open and close your hands together, like you're opening the Bible

Matthew 5:5

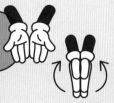

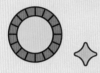

SERVE

JESUS LIVED THIS OUT... WHEN HE WASHED HIS DISCIPLES' FEET.

What's the dirtiest chore you've ever had to do? Draw a picture or write out the job you had to do below.

Chances are, you probably did that chore because you HAD to. When you follow Jesus, you might be surprised by what you'll find yourself WANTING to do!

Take this moment from Jesus' life that we find in John 13:1-17.

Jesus knew that He was about to go to the cross. He decided to gather His disciples together for a final meal and an important real-life lesson.

It's important to know that people back then didn't wear shoes like we do today. Some of them wore sandals, and some probably went barefoot. It's also important to know that the roads weren't paved. They were dusty and muddy. On top of that, the transportation of choice often included animals, so those roads were covered in... all sorts of things. GROSS! You get the picture. When people went inside somewhere, it was normal at the time for someone to have the job of washing people's feet.

Well, when the disciples showed up to Jesus' dinner, Jesus did something totally unexpected. Jesus Himself took off His outer robe. He tied a towel around His waist, grabbed some water, and started WASHING the disciples' dirty feet!

Jesus then told them:

"I have given you an example. You should do as I have done for you." — John 13:15

People don't like to do the dirty work. They'd rather have people do it for them. But the way of Jesus often looks like the way of opposites. As Jesus once said: **"Anyone who wants to be important among you must be your servant."** — Matthew 20:26

Humble or Not-So-Humble

#1 Think about what it means to put others before yourself and how Jesus showed humility. Circle the words that describe what being humble means.

#2 Think about some actions that focus only on yourself or putting others down. Cross out any words that DO NOT describe what it means to be humble.

When you think about Jesus' example of humility, some of the circled words probably come to mind. That's because Jesus constantly showed us what it looks like to be humble, and to think of others before ourselves. And now we can live that out with one another!

Giving

Caring

Selfish

Show-off

Understanding

Greedy

Thoughtful

Considerate

Helpful

Bragging

Generous

Rude

Mean

Kind

Bossy

Watch an episode of **SO&SO show** about this story!

Let's try something fun!

Here's what you'll need:

- ○ A timer
- ○ An opponent—like a grown-up, sibling, or friend
- ○ Two baking sheets (or big cutting boards—or even laundry baskets, or anything you can carry things in)
- ○ A piece of paper and something to write with

> There are lots of ways we can serve one another!

THINK ABOUT IT!

Why do you think Jesus thought it was important to serve others with humility?

What are some ways you might show humility in your own life?

Here's the challenge:

#1 You and your opponent will each get a baking sheet (or anything you can use to carry things).

#2 During the game, look around wherever you are for things that you could use to serve someone else. Think to yourself: "How could I use this to help someone?" Pile those things on top of your "serving tray."

#3 Set a three-minute timer and let the games begin!

#4 When time's up, sit together and explain your items to each other. You get a point for each item, as long as you can explain how you'd use that item to serve someone else.

#5 Count up your points and declare the winner!

HOW FOLLOWERS OF JESUS LIVED THIS OUT...

Let's check out some "humble service" in action.

One of the early followers of Jesus was a woman named Lydia. We can find her story in Acts 16:11-15. This passage describes what happened when Paul and his friends visited Philippi, the city where Lydia lived, to share the good news about Jesus.

Lydia was known for selling purple cloth. And she was good at it! She had earned enough money that she owned a house.

We also learn in verse 14 that Lydia was a **"worshiper of God"** —even though she hadn't yet heard about Jesus!

Paul and his friends went outside the city gate and down to the riverside. They found Lydia and several other women who had gathered there. Paul and his friends told the women all about Jesus—how He died and rose again to bring people back to God. Lydia believed, and she was baptized to show others that she trusted Jesus with her life. But the story didn't stop there!

Lydia immediately put Jesus' love into action with the way she served Paul and his friends. Lydia opened her home as a place for them to stay while they were in the city. After Paul and his friends left the city, Lydia continued to host the new church so the believers would have a place to meet together. We can imagine how Lydia used what she had to show love to many people there in Philippi.

We often think that service needs to include some sort of messy, dirty work. But service could look like welcoming people into your home, like Lydia did. Or it could mean just being there for someone who needs your help.

Grab some popcorn and your favorite movie snacks. It's time for a movie night!

Get ready to LIVE IT OUT by serving and hosting—like Lydia did!

HERE'S THE PLAN:

1 Let a sibling, friend, or other family member pick the movie.

2 Before the movie starts, create your own movie tickets and make them official! Add the date, movie name, and where you'll watch it.

3 Hand the movie tickets out to your guests. (This makes the at-home movie experience even more special!)

4 Once everyone is settled, take a minute to share Lydia's story. You can read it to them from pages 24-25, or ask someone else to read it to your audience. Explain how Lydia put her faith in Jesus, then served others by inviting them to use her home.

5 Then, start the movie.

6 Check in with everyone once or twice during the movie, asking, "Can I get you anything, like a glass of water or an extra blanket?"

7 After your movie night, come back and answer these questions on the next page.

ADMIT ONE

ADMIT ONE

After the movie:

How did it feel to serve by hosting a movie night?

_____

_____

_____

_____

How can you continue to serve the people around you?

_____

_____

_____

_____

Serving can be as simple as letting someone else choose the movie...
or passing out snacks before you get your own. Just like Lydia served
others by using her home, you can continue to LIVE IT OUT by
serving the people around you!

QUEST #1: SERVE ONE ANOTHER

1 DISCOVER

It takes humility to do the jobs no one really loves to do… and that's one way we can serve one another!

MESS QUEST: Pick a quest from the list that is NOT already your responsibility. Circle it, then move to step 2.

- → Take out the trash
- → Clean the bathroom
- → Wash the dishes
- → OTHER: Choose your own messy task and write it here:

_____

2 DRAW IT OUT

In the space below, draw the mess BEFORE you do the quest.

Then draw what it'll look like AFTER you clean it up.

3 LIVE IT OUT

LEVEL 1 Complete the Mess Quest that you picked.

LEVEL 2 Fill out this card and commit to doing this chore several times.

I will...

_____
(QUEST)

_____
(NUMBER)

times.

4 LOVE LIKE JESUS

Serving is one way we show love like Jesus did. Lydia served others by hosting them in her home. Jesus served others by washing His disciples' feet.

Pray to God

Talk to God about how you can find ways to serve every day.

SERVE

CONGRATULATIONS! YOU'VE EARNED THE

Serve One Another Badge

ROMANS 15:7

**Christ has accepted you.
So accept one another in order
to bring praise to God.**

QUEST
2

Accept

One Another

ACCEPT ONE ANOTHER

Who are your best friends? Take a second and write their names down on the short lines. Then, on the longer lines, write down some words that describe why they're such good friends.

_____   _____

_____   _____

_____   _____

_____   _____

_____   _____

It's nice to have friends who like the same things we do—movies, music, hobbies, sports, or even subjects in school. It's also nice to have friends who are totally different from us. We can learn so much from spending time with them! It's nice to have someone who shows up with a smile and your favorite snack when you're feeling sad. It's nice to have someone who accepts you for who you are.

That's a key part of sharing Jesus' love: accepting one another. The apostle Paul wrote about that to the followers of Jesus who were living in Rome:

Christ has accepted you. So accept one another in order to bring praise to God. — Romans 15:7

As you look at that verse, circle the word "accept." Then draw an arrow and write the word "welcome."

To accept someone is to welcome them. You might accept someone into your group of close friends. You might accept a new classmate or teammate. You might even accept a new baby brother or sister into your family.

Did you know that feeling accepted or welcomed is one of the most important feelings in the whole world? When people feel like they belong, they are more likely to have success in school and work, with relationships, and with their health.[1]

[1] National Library of Medicine: Sense of Belonging, Meaningful Daily Life Participation, and Well-Being: Integrated Investigation

So that brings up a good question: How can I help people feel like they belong?

Paul started with a simple idea: **"Christ has accepted you."** Back on the page with the verse, underline the word "Christ." Then draw an arrow and write "Jesus."

Jesus has accepted us. When Jesus died on the cross for our sins, He made a way for people to experience God's love and be accepted into a forever relationship with God.

Because of that, we can LIVE IT OUT and show Jesus' love to others by accepting them.

Make a welcome banner!

Create a welcome banner or sign for anyone who visits your home. Whether it's a friend, your parents' friends, a neighbor, or the mail carrier, you'll be ready to "wow" them and let them know you're glad they came!

DAY 1

01. Grab some paper and trace this banner shape on each sheet, then cut them out.

02. Write one letter on each banner shape to spell out a welcome greeting and decorate!

03. Use a hole punch or tape to add the banner shapes to a string and display near an entryway in your home.

Don't stop there!
Use any craft supplies you can find (think glitter, stickers, markers, or even leaves!) to make your banner stand out.

Write your own greeting!
It could be a fun song, a catchy poem, or even a short sentence that you can share anytime someone new shows up at your home.

WHAT JESUS SAID...

ACCEPT

When you start practicing what Jesus said, the way you live your life will change—which is really the point!

When Jesus was on Earth, His entire goal was to help people understand how much God loved them and wanted a relationship with them. Jesus also knew that for people to really know about God's love, they'd need to experience it and see it in action.

We know what Paul wrote: that love looks like accepting others. Jesus had something to say about that too:

"Blessed are those who are hungry and
thirsty for what is right.
They will be filled." — Matthew 5:6

On the surface, it might not seem like Jesus was talking about accepting one another. But accepting someone is a big part of doing what's right.

Think about it for a second. What makes you want to welcome someone into your group? Jot down a couple of ideas:

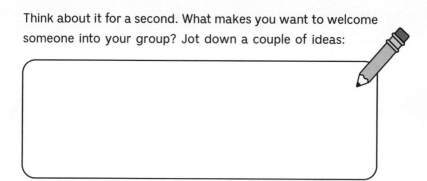

Jesus said that it's important for us to fix things that are broken... and make them right. We all know that there are things that are wrong in this world—things like fighting, or racism, or people not having enough food to eat or a place to live. When things are wrong in the world, followers of Jesus should work to make them better. And that goes for the way we connect with the people God has put in our lives. We should accept others and make them feel like they belong.

How do we know who deserves our acceptance? Well, if we follow the way of Jesus, it comes down to love.

If we work to make people feel accepted, we're following Jesus and showing His love to them.

You can LIVE IT OUT and help make things right by accepting and welcoming others... because God wants everyone to feel like they belong.

Who needs to be welcomed?

Think of someone who doesn't feel accepted. This could be a friend at school, someone you've heard about in the news, someone in your community, or someone else. Let's practice welcoming them!

Accepting people you see all the time:

Pick one way to welcome someone you see in your everyday life:

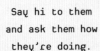

Say hi to them and ask them how they're doing.

Write a note with some encouraging words and give it to them.

Work with your parents to invite them to hang out.

Get to know three facts about them.

Share a snack or have a meal with them.

Ask, "Can we be friends?"

A prayer for someone you may never meet:

Dear God,
Today I'm thinking about

(_____ .)

(person or group of people)

I imagine sometimes they don't feel welcome...
or they might feel like they don't belong because

(_____ .)

(reason)

God, I know You created everyone and You
love everyone. Please help protect them from

(_____ .)

Please help them meet someone
who helps them to feel

(_____ .)

Please help them know they are loved and
welcomed so they can experience a full life.

If I ever meet anyone like them, remind me
that I can be a friend and I can accept them,
just like You do. In Jesus' name, amen.

JESUS LIVED THIS OUT... WHEN HE TOLD THE STORY OF THE GOOD SAMARITAN.

ACCEPT

People were always coming to Jesus with questions. One time, an expert in God's law asked Jesus, **"What must I do to receive eternal life?" — Luke 10:25**

Jesus asked the man what was written in God's law, and the man answered correctly—to love God and love your neighbor. But this law expert tried to trick Jesus with another question—asking, **"And who is my neighbor?" — Luke 10:29.** In other words, this man wanted to know WHO he was supposed to accept.

DAY 3

Jesus responded by telling a parable—a story that teaches an important lesson.

Jesus talked about a man who was traveling along the road when he was attacked by some thieves. Two different religious leaders walked by the man who had been robbed... but neither of them stopped to help.

Jesus then talked about another man who walked by—a Samaritan. In those days, Samaritans and Jewish people didn't get along... at all! To most Jewish people, Samaritans would not have been considered neighbors.

As Jesus told the story, the Samaritan stopped. He checked on the man, bandaged his wounds, and took him to a nearby place to stay. He offered to pay for any care the man might need.

The Samaritan went above and beyond to help the man who'd been robbed. The hero of the story—the person who showed love like Jesus—was the person who Jesus' listeners would have viewed as an enemy.

Jesus closed by saying, **"Go and do as he did."**
— Luke 10:37

Through this story, Jesus helped people see that God's love is for everyone! You can live out the love of Jesus by accepting others... and by loving your neighbor.

Who is my neighbor?

Did you know that anyone you're supposed to love is your neighbor—not just the people who live around you?

Take some time to think about all the different kinds of neighbors you have in the world.

You!

Close-By Neighbors
maybe someone next door
or someone you see every day

Not-As-Close Neighbors
maybe someone in your city
or someone you can visit by driving

Faraway Neighbors
maybe someone you can visit by flying
or someone across the country

Far, Far Away Neighbors
maybe someone in a country next door
or someone across the globe

Doodle some faces of different neighbors here in these windows.

They could be people you know, or people you haven't met yet!

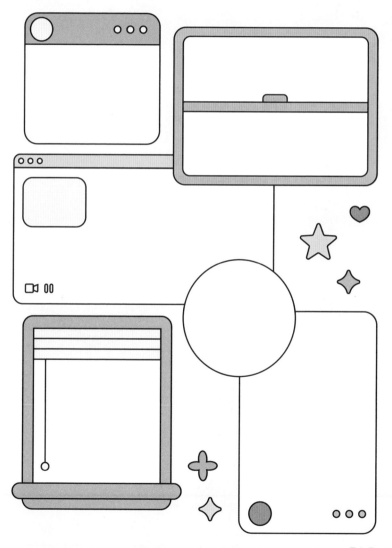

ACCEPT

HOW FOLLOWERS OF JESUS LIVED THIS OUT...

For thousands of years, Jesus-followers have been wondering about who should be welcomed and accepted.

There's actually a pretty wild story about this in the Bible. It involves people seeing visions... angels... animals being let down in a sheet (wait—what!?)... and one of Jesus' closest friends, Peter, going to visit a Roman commander named Cornelius.

One day, Cornelius was at his house when an angel told him to invite Peter over. So Cornelius sent some of his men to go get Peter. (Remember, he was a commander, so he got to tell people what to do.)

Meanwhile, Peter saw a vision—and this is where it gets wild.

Peter saw a sheet full of all kinds of animals. He heard a voice giving him permission to eat the kinds of animals he saw. This was a BIG DEAL because in Peter's life, you DID NOT eat certain animals because they were considered "unclean."

When Peter refused to consider those "unclean" animals to be food, the voice told him: **"Do not say anything is not pure that God has made 'clean.'"** **— Acts 10:15**

Did you catch that? The rules had just changed. Anything God had created and made clean was now supposed to be accepted as good. And if that was true about food... then it was also true about all people—even those who some people thought of as "not acceptable." This changed everything.

Peter and the men made it to Cornelius's house. There was just one problem. Peter was Jewish. Cornelius wasn't. And Jewish people normally weren't allowed to go to non-Jewish people's homes.

But because of what Peter learned from his vision of the animals in the sheet, he realized something new about his friendships with people who weren't like him. Peter said:

"I now realize how true it is that God treats everyone the same... He accepts people from every nation. He accepts anyone who has respect for him and does what is right." — Acts 10:34-35

Peter shared the message of Jesus with Cornelius, and Cornelius and his entire household chose to put their faith in Jesus!

We might think we know who God wants us to hang out with and accept. We might even wonder if people who aren't like us are worthy of our acceptance, our friendship, and our trust. But if we're going to LIVE IT OUT and love like Jesus, we need to accept one another. We can use wisdom to make sure the people we hang out with are safe. But we can choose to welcome others and accept them, whether they're like us or not.

 Watch an episode of about this story!

Show love to everyone!

If you want to accept people who are different from you, that starts with a choice. You need to choose to see them, recognize them, and make them feel welcome. That's how you love like Jesus!

Get creative and think of five ways you could show love to others—whoever they might be. Maybe it's by being a good listener, sharing your favorite snack, or just giving someone a smile when they need it most.

Come up with some other ideas, and fill them in below:

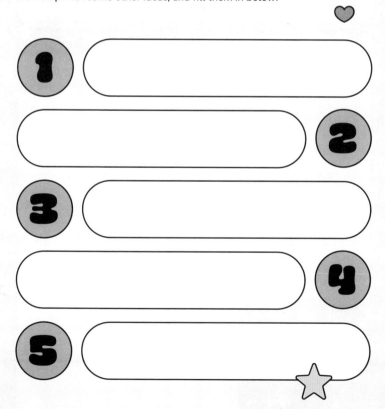

QUEST #2: ACCEPT ONE ANOTHER

1 DISCOVER

Discover an opportunity to use your voice!

Think of a person or a group of people in your life who aren't normally accepted. Keep them in mind as you work through this challenge.

2 WRITE IT OUT

Important people from world leaders to sports captains and artists have all used their voices to make sure others are accepted.

Now it's your turn. Write a short speech that inspires others to accept one another.

ACCEPT

_____

_____

_____

_____

_____

_____

_____

_____

_____

3 LIVE IT OUT

LEVEL 1 Practice your speech on your own.

LEVEL 2 Get dressed up, practice your speech, and deliver it to someone who has time to listen. Create a poster for your big speaking event. Be sure to put a date and time and invite anyone you know to hear your speech.

4 LOVE LIKE JESUS

When you want what's right… when it would be easier to let things stay wrong… that's a sign that you're ready to live like Jesus.

Talk About It

Find a trusted adult and tell them about some of the wrongs in the world you want to see made right.

WAY TO GO! YOU'VE EARNED THE

Accept One Another Badge

COLOSSIANS 3:13

Put up with one another. Forgive one another if you are holding something against someone. Forgive, just as the Lord forgave you.

QUEST 3

Forgive
One Another

FORGIVE ONE ANOTHER

FORGIVE

Do you have a backpack? Go ahead and grab it really quick.

Find some books and FILL that bag to the brim. Then put it on.

Now take a guess. How much do you think it weighs?

How long do you think you could carry that bag around without getting tired and sore?

Now, while wearing the backpack...

Try twisting
side to side.

Can you balance it
on one shoulder?

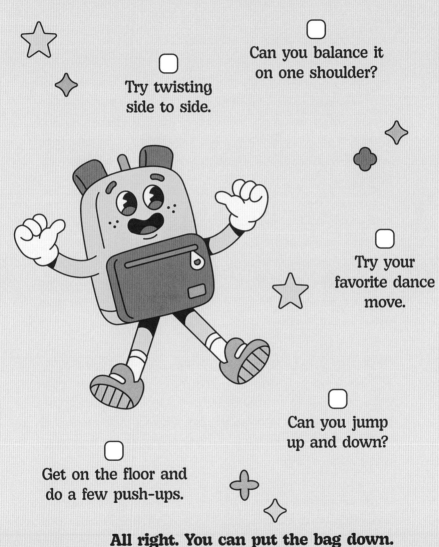

Try your
favorite dance
move.

Can you jump
up and down?

Get on the floor and
do a few push-ups.

All right. You can put the bag down.

Now imagine if you had to carry that bag around with you all the time and never take it off. At some point, your strength would run out. You'd get really sore. You'd want to toss that bag to the ground for some relief!

You see, you weren't meant to carry a heavy load like that. When you carry around feelings of anger, hurt, and frustration because of what others have done, it's like you're carrying a heavy bag everywhere you go. Instead, you can choose to let go of that heavy weight. With God's help, you can choose to forgive.

Paul wrote about forgiveness when he was helping new followers of Jesus understand how to live like Jesus. Paul wrote:

Forgive one another if you are holding something against someone. Forgive, just as the Lord forgave you. — Colossians 3:13

Forgiveness isn't easy. To be honest, it's one of the most difficult ways to show Jesus' love to others, and you might need an adult to help you. But we can choose to forgive because Jesus has forgiven US. Jesus loved us so much that He died on the cross for us, to pay the price for the things we've done wrong.

When you forgive, your world gets a little lighter. It doesn't mean that what the person did is okay. It doesn't mean that the person won't have to face the consequences for what they've done wrong. And it doesn't mean that you need to put yourself in a situation where you're scared or could get hurt. It just means that you no longer hold on to the anger or hurt they've caused you.

You can choose to let it go.

FORGIVE

WHAT JESUS SAID...

Jesus reimagined what our life could look like if we choose to follow Him. And forgiveness can be a powerful way for us to show Jesus' love.

Jesus talked about an idea that can help us forgive:

"Blessed are those who show mercy.
    They will be shown mercy." — Matthew 5:7

Have you heard that word before—mercy? It means that you show love or compassion to someone who's in trouble. Chances are you've experienced mercy at some point in your life.

Maybe a parent helped you clean up the spaghetti you spilled on the floor instead of getting frustrated with you.

Maybe your sibling still invited you to play a game even though you broke their favorite toy.

Maybe a teammate said something to encourage you after you missed a shot or struck out.

When someone does something to hurt someone else, of course there should be consequences. Cheat on a test? Get a failing grade. Trip someone on the playground? Sit out from participating. Talk about someone behind their back? Lose friends.

But you have a choice in how you respond to the person who made an unwise, bad choice that may have hurt you.

You could get angry and keep thinking over and over about what they've done. You could even spend your time imagining what you'd like to do to get back at them.

OR... you can choose to show mercy.
You can choose to forgive.
You can choose to let it go.

Forgiveness can be an amazing way for you to show Jesus' love. At the same time, it can also help you heal on the inside (which is just as important). And remember, you don't have to do it alone. God is always with you as you try to LIVE IT OUT!

What's in your control?

There are things you have control over, and there are things you can let go of because you DON'T have control.

Draw a line from each star to a circle to show what you can and can't control.

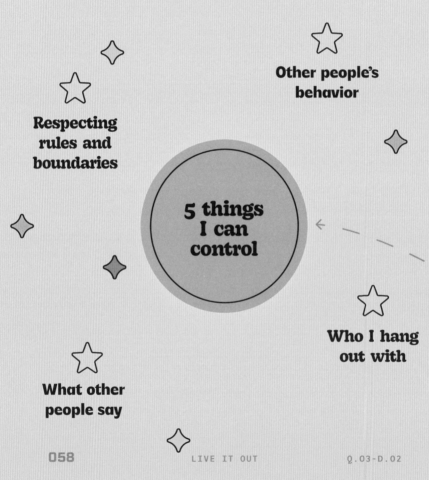

Other people's behavior

Respecting rules and boundaries

5 things I can control

Who I hang out with

What other people say

What I say to others

The weather

5 things I can't control

Taking care of myself

What other people think

Time

My actions

DAY 2

JESUS LIVED THIS OUT... WHEN HE FORGAVE HIS FRIEND PETER.

FORGIVE

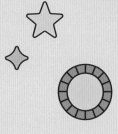

DAY 3

Remember when we talked about how Jesus washed His friends' feet? Well, there was something else that happened that same evening.

Jesus told His disciples that they would all turn away from Him. Peter couldn't believe it! He spoke up and said that he would never leave Jesus' side. But Jesus knew differently.

Jesus told Peter:

"Before the rooster crows, you will say three times that you don't know me." — Matthew 26:34

When Jesus was betrayed and arrested, most of the disciples ran and hid. But Peter stayed close enough to watch what was happening. Three times, people came up to Peter and asked him if he knew Jesus. Peter was scared, and so each time, he said he didn't know who Jesus was. As Peter denied knowing Jesus the third time, a rooster crowed. Peter realized that he had broken his promise.

Fast-forward to when Jesus died on the cross, then came back to life. One morning, Jesus appeared to His disciples on the beach after they had been out fishing for the night. Peter must have wondered how Jesus would treat him after what he had done.

Jesus could have ignored Peter. He could have told Peter that He was disappointed in him, or said that he was no longer a disciple.

Instead... Jesus FORGAVE Peter.

In fact, Jesus told Peter that he would be the leader of the growing community of Jesus-followers that would eventually become the church. About six weeks later, Peter shared the truth of Jesus to thousands of people who had gathered in Jerusalem for the feast of Pentecost.

Jesus restored His friendship with Peter by choosing forgiveness. And we can follow Jesus' example. We can offer that same kind of forgiveness to people who have wronged us.

So, what does this mean for us? It means that, just like Jesus forgave Peter, we can forgive others too.

Take out a phone or tablet (with permission from a grown-up!) and scan these QR codes. These songs are all about God's forgiveness and love.

All of the Ways

Lift My Voice

When you listen to the songs...

 Sing along!

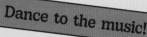 Think about a time when someone forgave you.

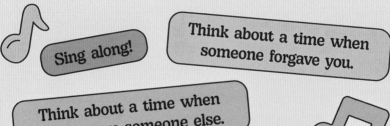 Think about a time when you forgave someone else.

Dance to the music!

After listening, come back and share your thoughts here!

Which song did you like better and why?

_____

_____

_____

_____

_____

How do you think these songs connect with Peter's story?

_____

_____

_____

_____

_____

DAY 3

FORGIVE

JESUS TAUGHT HOW HIS FOLLOWERS COULD LIVE THIS OUT...

Watch an episode of THE **SO&SO** *show* about this story!

DAY 4

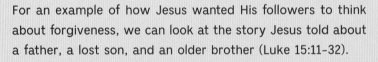

For an example of how Jesus wanted His followers to think about forgiveness, we can look at the story Jesus told about a father, a lost son, and an older brother (Luke 15:11-32).

In those days, fathers passed down their money and things they owned to their sons when they died. But, as Jesus explained, the younger son didn't want to wait. He went to his father and asked to have his inheritance right then and there.

The father loved his son and gave him what he wanted... and the son took off and partied it up. But eventually the money completely ran out. The son had no choice but to feed pigs and eat the food scraps meant for them. The son finally decided to return home, beg for forgiveness, and ask if his father would hire him as a worker.

When the father saw his son coming in the distance, he came running! He gave his son a giant hug. He forgave him and welcomed him back home. He even threw a giant party to celebrate.

The older son wasn't happy about this. He didn't want to go to the party, because he didn't think his brother should be forgiven. But the father explained:

"'We had to celebrate and be glad. This brother of yours was dead. And now he is alive again. He was lost. And now he is found.'" — Luke 15:32

There are times when you might feel like the younger son in the story. You might need to say you're sorry for what you've done. You might need to ask for forgiveness.

There are also times when you might feel like the older son. You might be angry about the wrong things someone else has done. You might not want to offer forgiveness.

The first Jesus-followers had the chance to learn from Jesus' teachings and live them out. And we have the same chance today. We can take our cue from Jesus... and forgive.

All right—let's jump into the shoes of the two brothers in the story Jesus told about the lost son.

Let's see how differently these two brothers might have felt and acted!

#1
Imagine you're the older brother.

Answer these questions in the blanks of the shoe print on this page:

➡ How did the older brother feel when his little brother came back after blowing all that money? Maybe a little annoyed? Or even jealous?

➡ How do you think he could have acted instead?

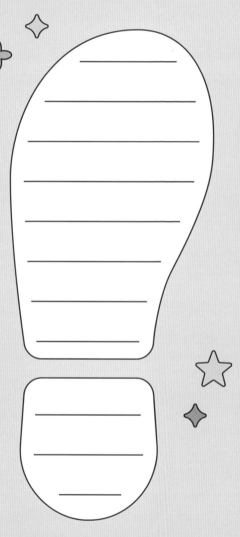

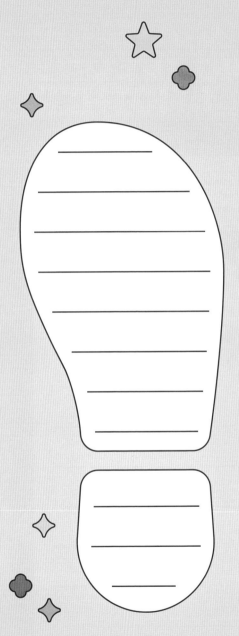

#2
Now, picture yourself as the younger brother who came back home.

Answer these questions in the blanks of the shoe print on this page:

➡ What do you think was going through the younger brother's mind in this story? Do you think he was nervous? Maybe even scared?

➡ How do you think he felt when his dad threw him a huge party instead of getting angry?

QUEST #3: FORGIVE ONE ANOTHER

1 DISCOVER

Think about this: have you ever had to be forgiven? If so, what were some feelings you felt? How do you think others feel when they want to be forgiven?

2 ACT IT OUT

We've been talking about how forgiveness can lighten your load.

Find a friend, give this scenario a try, and see how it feels to practice forgiving someone—even if it's just pretend for now!

PERSON 1: Hi! I accidentally broke your gaming system. Please forgive me.

PERSON 2 (YOU!):

_____

_____

_____

_____

_____

_____

_____

FORGIVE

3 LIVE IT OUT

LEVEL 1 In the space on the right, write down the names of people you have forgiven or are working on forgiving.

LEVEL 2 Think about someone who you want to forgive—maybe someone whose name you just wrote down. Ask God to help you forgive them.

_____

_____

_____

_____

_____

4 LOVE LIKE JESUS

Forgiveness isn't always easy, but it's always worth it.

Memorize this verse to help you practice forgiveness:

Hear from God

Put up with one another. Forgive one another if you are holding something against someone. Forgive, just as the Lord forgave you. (Colossians 3:13)

CONGRATULATIONS! YOU'VE EARNED THE

Forgive One Another Badge

ROMANS 15:14

You are filled with knowledge and able to teach one another.

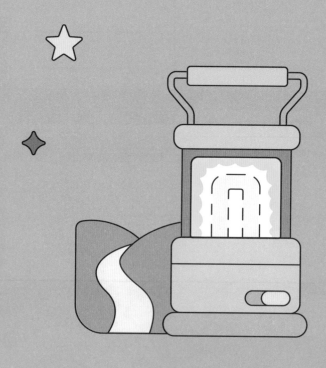

QUEST 4

QUEST **4**

Teach

One
Another

TEACH

Question for you: who's your favorite teacher? Jot down their name:

Now, out of all the teachers you've had in your life, why did that particular teacher come to mind as your favorite? Write a few ideas below.

DAY 1

Our favorite teachers usually have some things in common:

- ➡ They know what they're talking about and work really hard.
- ➡ They make learning fun.
- ➡ They inspire us to learn and grow.
- ➡ Most importantly, they're kind and actually care about what's happening in our lives.

The best teachers see their job as a way to love others. They love their students and want to see them succeed—not only in class, but in life.

It shouldn't come as a surprise, then, that Paul talked about teaching as way to show Jesus' love. Paul wrote this to the Jesus-followers in Rome:

You are filled with knowledge and able to teach one another. — Romans 15:14

It's like Paul was saying:

- ➡ "You have what it takes."
- ➡ "You're loving others like Jesus."
- ➡ "You've been living it out!"
- ➡ "Now, go show your love by teaching others how to do the same."

Ever since Jesus was first here on Earth, people have loved like Jesus by teaching others about Jesus. And maybe now it's your turn. You see, teaching others about Jesus is a great way to LIVE IT OUT.

Now, you might be thinking... "Wait. WHAT? Me, a teacher?"

- ➡ "I'm too young."
- ➡ "I don't know enough about Jesus."
- ➡ "I'm just a kid."

Well, guess what: you probably know more than you think! And beyond that, being able to teach others about Jesus is way more than knowing a bunch of facts about Jesus. When you share Jesus' love by living it out, you can be a great teacher—no matter how old you might be.

Interview an adult:
On your next walk or ride together, or at dinner...

Start the conversation!

Ask your grown-up to share about their favorite subject and their favorite teacher when they were in school.

Ask them:

What is something you remember learning when you were my age?

Share your experience!

Then share about your favorite subject in school and teach them something you recently learned.

Your very own show!

Get into character, throw on a made-up costume, and pretend to be a vlogger teaching others about something that's important to you. Perform your "video" for your parent or an adult you trust.

[SCRIPT] Hello, and welcome to my channel! If you're new here, welcome back! Did you know that I'm not too young to teach others about the things I know and love? That's actually a way that I can show love to others.

Today, I'll be teaching you all about _____
_____.

Here are three facts about it:
1. _____.
2. _____.
3. _____.
One thing I find fascinating about _____
is _____.

Thanks for watching my channel! To learn more about
_____, don't forget to like and subscribe!

Mix it up!

➜ Do your "video" as a "get ready with me."

➜ Do your "video" as a challenge show.

➜ Do your "video" as a documentary.

➜ Do your "video" while dancing.

➜ Throw in a fake giveaway in your "video."

WHAT JESUS SAID...

TEACH

Great teachers lead by example. They teach things that are true about their own life. If they're hard workers, have a sense of humor, and are genuinely kind, chances are they'll be teachers who will top all sorts of students' best teacher lists.

Paul told the Jesus-followers in Rome that he knew they would be able to teach one another. That means they could teach people by telling them important things about Jesus. But they could also teach people with their actions.

The same thing is true for us today. The best way to teach others about the love of Jesus is to be *filled* with the love of Jesus. Remember, Jesus reimagined what our life could look like if we choose to follow Him.

Jesus said this:

> "Blessed are those whose hearts are pure.
>   They will see God." — Matthew 5:8

The word "hearts" here means more than just the heart beating in your chest. It describes your whole, entire self. It means your thoughts, feelings, emotions, and all the things that make you... you.

In other words, it's like Jesus was saying, "Blessed are those whose LIVES are pure."

When you trust Jesus with your life, you don't just follow Jesus sometimes. You don't act one way around your friends who also follow Jesus, and then a different way around everyone else. You follow Jesus wherever you are, whoever you're with, every single day.

If your heart is pure, then the things you say and do will line up with who you are as a person who trusts and follows Jesus. And other people will see God's love through you!

That's where the teaching comes in. You can teach with the way you act and the choices you make each day. You can live as an example of what it means to follow Jesus. You can LIVE IT OUT.

Play a game of charades!

At home, act out these phrases about teaching someone something.

#1
Write these phrases on pieces of paper.

#2
Ball them up and put them in a cup or a hat.

#3
Pick one and act it out to someone who can try to guess what you're doing!

Teaching someone how to tie their shoe

Teaching a chef's class how to cook a meal

Teaching someone how to do their hair as a YouTube tutorial video

Teaching an adult how to do a popular dance (you pick the dance!)

Teaching a baby how to walk

Teaching an astronaut how to walk on the moon

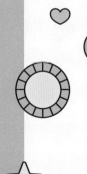

TEACH

JESUS LIVED THIS OUT... WHEN HE WAS TEMPTED IN THE WILDERNESS.

Jesus didn't just talk about living with a heart that's pure. He lived this out in His own life.

There's a moment from Jesus' life that lets us see just how much integrity He had... when God's Spirit led Him into the wilderness.

This wasn't some desert spa where Jesus ate all sorts of delicious food, hung out by the pool, and played tennis. NOPE! What Jesus experienced was quite the opposite.

Jesus was in the desert for 40 days. And while He was there, He didn't eat a single thing. On top of that, the devil tested Him.

First, the devil tempted Jesus to use His power over creation to turn a stone into bread. Jesus had grown up learning the truth from the Jewish Scriptures. He also knew God's heart. So He replied to the devil with words that originally came from the book of Deuteronomy:

DAY 3

"It is written, 'Man must not live only on bread.'" — Luke 4:4

Next, according to Luke's account, the devil promised Jesus authority over all the kingdoms of the world, if Jesus would only bow down and worship him. But Jesus knew He was to worship God and God alone. He quoted what he knew from Scripture in the book of Deuteronomy:

"It is written, 'Worship the Lord your God. He is the only one you should serve.'" — Luke 4:8

The devil thought he'd try one last time. From the top part of the temple, the devil suggested that Jesus should jump off, because God would send angels to rescue Him. Again, Jesus quoted from Deuteronomy:

"Scripture says, 'Do not test the Lord your God.'" — Luke 4:12

Jesus stayed true to what He believed about God and about God's plan for His life.

Like Jesus did, we can look to the words of Scripture and find out what's true. Then we'll have everything we need not only to live the way Jesus taught us, but to teach others about what God wants for their life too.

It's good for us to practice finding God's wisdom in the Bible.

On the next page, there's a list of topics that people might need help with—like being kind, dealing with worry, or standing up for what's right.

We've got some verses from the Bible that talk about those exact things. Can you match the right verse to the right topic after looking them up in your Bible (or Bible app)?

Here's an example:

Let's say the topic is "being kind." We could match it with Ephesians 4:32a (the first part), which says, **"Be kind and tender to one another."** See how that works?

Bonus! Want to take it to the next level?

Try memorizing one of the verses you match up. Share it with someone this week who could use some encouragement!

Watch an episode of **THE SO & SO show** about this story!

EPHESIANS 4:32A

TRUSTING GOD

PHILIPPIANS 4:6-7

FORGIVING OTHERS

GALATIANS 6:9

DEALING WITH WORRY

COLOSSIANS 3:13

STANDING UP FOR WHAT'S RIGHT

DAY 3

PROVERBS 3:5-6

BEING KIND

HOW FOLLOWERS OF JESUS LIVED THIS OUT...

Before we get started today, think about these two questions.

What are some things you can do now that you couldn't do when you were younger?

What are some things you still can't wait to do because you're not old enough yet?

DAY 4

It's hard to wait to drive a car or go on a super-tall roller coaster. But even right now, when you're young, you can still do some amazing things. You can teach others about things you already know and are able to do now. And one of those things might be what you know about following Jesus.

In Acts 16, we find out that Paul met a young man named Timothy. Paul became a mentor to Timothy. He taught Timothy all about not only following Jesus, but teaching others about living for Jesus too.

Eventually, Paul put Timothy in charge of an entire community of Jesus-followers. But it seems like Timothy was struggling with his confidence to lead this group well... so Paul wrote a letter to Timothy to encourage him.

Paul told Timothy:

Don't let anyone look down on you because you are young. Set an example for the believers in what you say and in how you live. Also set an example in how you love and in what you believe. Show the believers how to be pure. — 1 Timothy 4:12

Just like Timothy, you might feel like you're too young to teach anyone about anything. But there's something really important that you can do. You can set an example and teach others with the way you live.

With God's help, you can set an example of living with kindness, honesty, grit, and creativity. And as you choose to follow Jesus by showing His love, other people will be able to see what God is doing IN you. That may inspire them to trust God and follow Jesus with their life too.

Remember, your actions can lead others in a BIG way.

Even though there are things you can't do quite yet, there are so many incredible things you CAN do.

Remember when we mentioned roller coasters? They're full of twists and turns, high points, and crazy drops. Our lives can be a bit like a roller coaster too. The cool thing is, no matter where we are on the ride, we get to show other people what it means to be a follower of Jesus with the way we live. That's true whether we're having the best day, or feeling like we're in a dip.

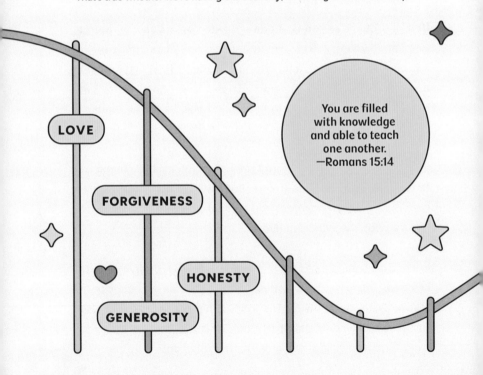

LOVE

FORGIVENESS

HONESTY

GENEROSITY

> You are filled with knowledge and able to teach one another.
> —Romans 15:14

Look at the words on the roller coaster. How can you can live them out? And how can you set an example for those around you?

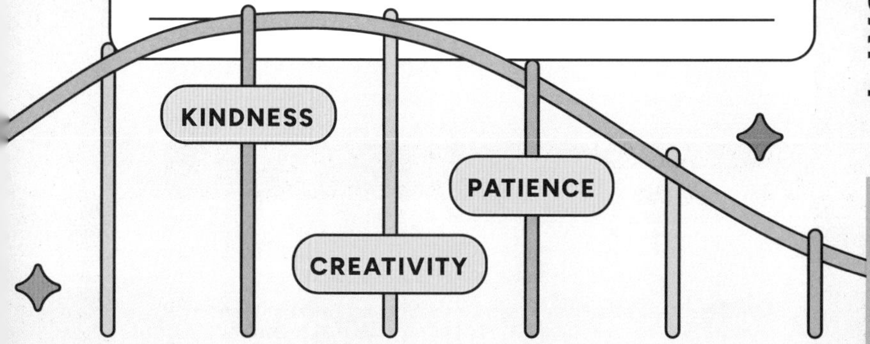
KINDNESS
PATIENCE
CREATIVITY

DAY 4

QUEST #4: TEACH ONE ANOTHER

1 DISCOVER

Teaching doesn't just look like standing in front of a classroom. Teaching shows up in different ways. Discover your teaching style by trying this Quest!

2 MAP IT OUT

Today you get to practice teaching someone how to love like Jesus. Go to each location on the map. Try the teaching style. And rate how much you enjoyed that teaching style by filling in the stars.

3 LIVE IT OUT

Which teaching style did you give the most stars? Now, use that teaching style and go teach your adult one thing you've learned while doing this book.

4 LOVE LIKE JESUS

There are lots of ways to teach others how to live like Jesus. The best way is to practice what we preach and to be an example for others.

DAY 5

Live for God

Think about it: What's one way you can live and love like Jesus this week?

Megaphone Mountain: Tell ☆☆☆☆☆
Front Stage Lake: Act ☆☆☆☆☆
Go-Getter Gorge: Do ☆☆☆☆☆
Artist Island: Draw ☆☆☆☆☆

MEGAPHONE MOUNTAIN

GO-GETTER GORGE

FRONT STAGE LAKE

ARTIST ISLAND

DO Choose a way to either serve, accept, forgive, or teach like Jesus. Now go do it!

TELL Write a speech teaching others how to love like Jesus. Include three action steps for them to take.

ACT Create a play with props and costumes. Write out a short scene about a problem one person could help someone else solve. Act out how to love like Jesus.

DRAW Create a masterpiece that shows how to love like Jesus. Draw, paint, build, sculpt, design, or engineer it! As you create, think of words that describe Jesus: Like love, forgiveness, kindness, etc.

NICE WORK! YOU'VE EARNED THE Teach One Another Badge

**If possible, live in peace
with everyone. Do that
as much as you can.**

QUEST 5

QUEST

5

Live in

Peace

With One
Another

LIVE IN PEACE WITH ONE ANOTHER

We've looked at a lot of different ideas that Paul shared in his letters about how we can LIVE IT OUT and love like Jesus. Let's look at one more.

In Paul's letter to the Romans, he wrote:

If possible, live in peace with everyone. Do that as much as you can. — Romans 12:18

Let's break that down together.

Paul started off by saying, "If possible."

If something is possible, that means it *could* happen. That doesn't mean it always *will* happen. In the verse above, next to the phrase "if possible," draw an arrow and jot down, "COULD be!"

Now let's look at the phrase "live in peace."

Sometimes we might think that *peace* means having a calm feeling without a care in the world. Or we might think that peace means that we never argue or disagree with anyone.

But when you LIVE in peace, that means you work for peace. You choose to show love because you care more about the other person than you care about winning.

Go back to the verse and circle the word "live." Draw an arrow and write "take action!" Circle the word "peace." Draw an arrow and write "work hard to get along."

It can be really hard to get along with some people, especially when what they're doing is causing harm. Some arguments are important enough to have in order to express what you know is right. It could even be that "living in peace" means walking away from the person and creating space between you and them. But if peace is possible, we should work to get along.

And who should we try to get along with? Go back to the verse and circle "everyone."

If that sounds tough, you're right. It IS tough. But God will be with you, and you have the Bible and this field guide to help! In the days ahead, we'll look at some different ideas and examples to help you figure out how to make peace.

Imagine this: you're in a tricky situation with a friend who just won't listen.

You're trying to explain your side of the story, but your friend keeps interrupting you. It's really frustrating.

What could "living in peace" look like at that moment? Could it mean walking away for a bit? How would you handle it?

WHAT JESUS SAID...

It makes sense that Paul said we should make peace with one another. After all, Paul was following Jesus' lead.

Jesus Himself said it this way:

"Blessed are those who make peace.
    They will be called children of God."
— Matthew 5:9

Jesus made it clear: His followers should be peacemakers.

That doesn't mean that you should ignore the problems you have with someone and pretend they don't exist. It means that if you do have an argument or a problem with someone—especially someone you care about—it's important to do the hard work to make things right in your relationship.

Now, as you know, being a peacemaker isn't easy. When people aren't getting along, emotions can run wild. People might feel hurt, angry, or sad... or all three at the same time!

If you're feeling those feelings, you might need to find peace within yourself before you try to make peace with others. Take time to pray and ask God to give you wisdom about what to do or say. You also might ask for advice from a friend, teacher, parent, or other trusted adult.

With God's help, we can take the first step to make peace with someone... because that's what God did for us.

God made peace with us.

We've all done things that are wrong—things that break our relationship with God and others. Out of a great love, God chose to send Jesus to rescue us. And because of Jesus, we become children of God! We are part of God's family, and we know that God will always be with us.

God's amazing love can inspire us to LIVE IT OUT by making peace with the people in our lives.

Is there someone who you could try to make peace with?

Let's get real with our emotions here! When you think about making peace with that person, is there anything that bubbles up inside you? Draw some emoji faces in these bubbles to show how that makes you feel.

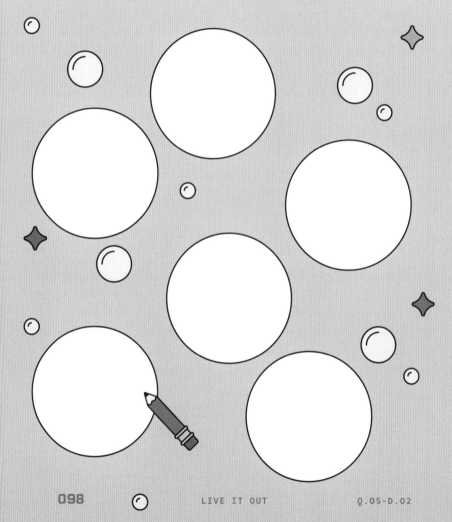

Now, use this bubble to talk to God about it. Ask God for help! You could write something like, "God, give me wisdom and courage to have a conversation with [Person's Name Here]." This is your reminder to pray before you take action.

Here's another bubble. This one's for you to take action! Write down one simple thing you can do to start making peace. Maybe it's saying, "I'm sorry," or asking advice from a teacher or trusted adult.

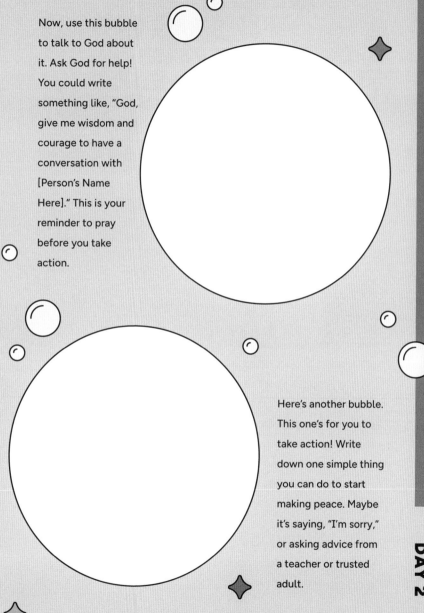

DAY 2

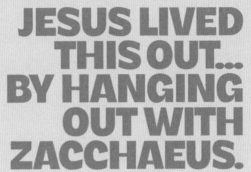

JESUS LIVED THIS OUT... BY HANGING OUT WITH ZACCHAEUS.

Jesus shared lots of ideas that challenged people and made them think about a different way to live. Perhaps one of His most challenging statements was this one:

"Love your enemies. Pray for those who hurt you."
— Matthew 5:44

We can see how Jesus lived out this big idea with the way He treated a man named Zacchaeus.

Zacchaeus—let's call him Zac—was a tax collector. He took taxes from the Jewish people to pay the Romans who were in charge. It was like he was working for the enemy. On top of that, tax collectors had a reputation for taking more money than they should... and keeping the extra for themselves.

As we read in Luke 19, Jesus was traveling toward Jerusalem for Passover. On the journey, He stopped in the town of Jericho. Meanwhile, Zac found out that Jesus was headed his way and decided to go have a look for himself. Zac climbed into a tree to make sure he could see above the crowds.

Well, Jesus stopped walking, looked up into the tree, and called for Zac by name!

Jesus said:

"Zacchaeus, come down at once. I must stay at your house today." — Luke 19:5

Sure enough, Jesus went to visit Zac. He wasn't worried about what the other people might think—even though they saw Zac as an enemy.

Zac was so moved by Jesus' love that he promised to give his money to people in need. He also promised to repay the people he had cheated—four times more than he took!

Jesus gave us an incredible example of how we can live out His love. We can make peace with people who we might consider our enemies—or at least people we don't always get along with. And that kind of love can change the world!

Think about how people in your life might like different things or think in different ways.

For example, think about someone in your classroom... a neighbor... a teammate... or a YouTuber. Use the puzzle pieces below to write their names and explain how they're different from you. Maybe they look different, enjoy different things, like to eat different foods, are more adventurous, or are more chill.

If you look at these puzzle pieces, you can tell that each piece is pretty different. But yet they all fit together to make a puzzle!

Jesus loved hanging out with all kinds of people—even Zacchaeus, the tax collector, who wasn't exactly everyone's favorite. Even when we don't see eye to eye, we can still live more like Jesus by making peace with one another!

If possible, live in peace with everyone. Do that as much as you can. Romans 12:18

HOW FOLLOWERS OF JESUS LIVED THIS OUT...

Did you know that Paul wasn't always a follower of Jesus? You could even say he was an ENEMY of Jesus.

Paul (also known as Saul) had started out as a religious leader called a Pharisee. Pharisees wanted to make sure that people followed the Jewish laws exactly.

Since Jesus came to fulfill and reimagine those laws, the Pharisees felt like He was destroying everything they stood for. So Paul made it his mission to stop everything and anything having to do with Jesus.

When Paul was on his way to Damascus to do just that, Jesus sent a bright light that stopped him right in his tracks. Jesus had chosen Paul to share His love with people and let them know how to follow Him. In an instant, Paul's life changed completely!

But Paul had a reputation that would be hard for him to shake. Eventually, Paul made his way to Jerusalem to join the rest of the Jesus-followers, but they wouldn't accept him. They couldn't believe that Paul had changed and was now a follower of Jesus.

This is where a man named Barnabas stepped in to make peace between Paul and the other believers. (Remember, Paul was also known as Saul.)

Barnabas took [Saul] to the apostles. He told them about Saul's journey. He said that Saul had seen the Lord. He told how the Lord had spoken to Saul. Barnabas also said that Saul had preached without fear in Jesus' name in Damascus. — Acts 9:27

After that, the believers accepted Paul. They even helped Paul get started on the mission that Jesus had given him on the road to Damascus. Paul went from enemy to friend, all because Barnabas took a risk to make peace.

God might be prompting us to do the same thing—to make peace for someone else. God can give us the courage, strength, and wisdom to do that. God can even bring people alongside us who can help us LIVE IT OUT!

Let's imagine this!

Here's what you'll need:

○ A flashlight
(a phone flashlight works!)

○ A dark room or closet

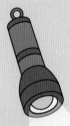

Here's the challenge:

#1 At home, head to a dark room or closet with your flashlight.

#2 Let's put ourselves in Paul's shoes. Turn off that light and sit for a moment. Think about how Paul was suddenly blinded by the bright light when Jesus spoke to him.

#3 Now, turn on your flashlight! Think about how Paul was changed by the light of Jesus on his way to Damascus, just like that. And then Paul went from an enemy to a friend of the other believers... because Barnabas took a risk to speak up for him.

Watch an episode of
THE SO & SO show
about this story!

Barnabas played a huge role in helping Paul make peace with the other believers. He LIVED IT OUT!

Who are the friends and people in your life who help you LIVE IT OUT?

QUEST #5: LIVE IN PEACE WITH ONE ANOTHER

1 DISCOVER

As we've just discovered, you can choose to make peace with others.

Here's a fun challenge you can do alone, with a family member, or with a friend.

2 MOVE IT OUT

Make a mini obstacle course—either inside or outside.

BUILD!
Get creative with your obstacle course by using chairs, pillows, cones, or chalk outdoors. Add zig-zag paths, crawl under a table, jump over hurdles, or build a maze with dominoes, blocks, or plastic cups. Have fun with it!

RULES!
Grab a cup of water and carry it through the course without spilling. (For a smaller maze, try closing your eyes and moving a pencil or straw through it without knocking anything down.)

RUN!
Time yourself or race against a family member or friend. As you balance the cup of water, think about how we often have to slow down and be careful if we want to make peace.

BONUS! Try your obstacle course again... but add another challenge, like running backward or holding a larger cup.

3 LIVE IT OUT

LEVEL 1 Whether you completed the challenge alone or with someone else, talk about it! Did you have to focus more on certain parts of the course?

LEVEL 2 Think about how you want to live more like Jesus this week. Share your ideas with a trusted adult.

4 LOVE LIKE JESUS

Following Jesus means staying focused on what's true, especially when life gets tough. Maybe you're navigating challenges with friends, or a sibling, or just trying to do the right thing when it's not easy. Jesus' example will always show us the way! When we follow His example, we can make peace with one another.

LIVE IN PEACE

Hear from God

Take a few minutes to think about the stories and ideas from the Bible that we discussed in this section. Which one stood out to you the most? Day 1, Day 2, or Day 3 or Day 4? Why? Grab a piece of paper and write about it!

AWESOME! YOU'VE EARNED THE
Live in Peace With One Another Badge

WELL, YOU DID IT!

You made it all the way to the end of this field guide. Hopefully you have a better idea of what it can look like for YOU to LIVE IT OUT!

You've traveled through five big ideas that can show up when you choose to follow Jesus with your whole life:

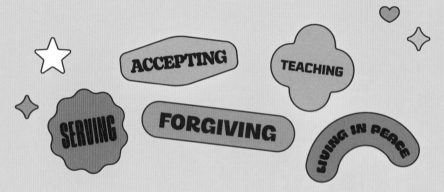

ACCEPTING
TEACHING
SERVING
FORGIVING
LIVING IN PEACE

All of these are based on what Jesus said is most important: "LOVE ONE ANOTHER."

But here's the thing. Even though you've made it to the end of this book, you're actually just getting started. Now it's time to put it all into practice!

If you're not sure where to start, start with the people closest to you and go from there. This is a journey that doesn't end. There's always an adventure around the corner.